W0013596

Vegetarian Soups and Sauces

- A Collection of Old-Time Recipes using No Meat -

BY

Ivan Baker

British Library Cataloguing-in-Publication Data
A catalogue record for this book is available from
the British Library

SOUP

" If only we had some olive-oil," runs the Spanish folk song, " a few pimentos, and a little salt, we could make una sopa " : a soup !

Like most Spanish dishes, it would begin in the casserole, the sliced pimentos being gently sautéd in the olive-oil before the water was added. A diligent search would be made, meanwhile, for the inevitable garlic, which the song seems to have taken for granted. Whether a thick, clear, or crème soup resulted would depend upon the proportions of the ingredients and the manner of their blending.

Skilfully prepared, and served piping hot with a chic contrasting garnish, such a soup, given a high sounding French title, might well conceal its humble origin.

The whole art of meatless soup making, indeed, consists in isolating the fresh, delicate flavours of simple vegetables, or the essence of pulses such as pea and bean. To these are added the zest of flavouring herbs and spices, subtle seasonings, and the strength of mushrooms, onions, or Marmite. The soup is bound, if so desired, with egg yolks and enriched with milk, cream, and butter.

Garnishes are important, often giving to soups their specific character and never failing to impart, if well chosen, novelty and added nutriment. With cream soups and purées serve a crisp cereal garnish, or dainty crackers—of the " cheese biscuit " class, or dainty croûtons. Clear soups are enhanced by the addition of little quenelles, ravioli, and the Italian pastes.

The well-tried recipes in this section contain the

favourite features of popular and exotic soups, modified, varied, or improved to suit requirements of meatless cookery. A very brief study of particular recipes selected for making up will give the necessary cue to their distinctive flavour and method of preparation.

The resultant quantity of soup is not based upon a given number of portions, as in the case of the other recipes. Cooks will therefore calculate the amount of ingredients for the quantity of soup required.

Serve soups whenever possible in attractive soup cups, or small bowls rather than in vast Victorian soup plates.

Mushroom Bisque

¾ lb. mushrooms	1 quart milk
1 tablespoon grated raw onion	Yolk of 1 egg
	1 teaspoon Marmite
1 oz. butter	Salt
1 dessertspoon flour	Paprika

Clean, peel, and slice the mushrooms. Toss them in the melted butter for ten minutes. Add the flour previously blended with a little cold milk. Then add a quart of hot milk, and the grated onion. Let simmer for twenty minutes.

Remove from the fire, stir in the beaten yolk of egg, and add the Marmite and seasoning. Reheat without boiling, and serve.

Mulligatawny (1)

1 pint curried vegetables	1 small sweet apple
1 oz. butter	3 bay leaves
1 teaspoon curry powder	2 oz. grated fresh coco-nut
1 small onion	1 tablespoon fruit chutney

Soak the coco-nut in half a cup of boiling water. Slice and fry the onion in the butter, adding the curry powder when slightly coloured, and cook two minutes more. Add three pints of vegetable stock or water, the curried vegetables, chopped onion, chopped apple, bay leaves, and chutney. Let the whole simmer for forty-five minutes, remove the bay leaves, and add the coconut liquor.

Serve hot with boiled rice.

Mulligatawny (2)

½ lb. carrots
½ lb. yellow swedes
2 leeks
2 onions
1 tart apple
2 oz. cooked grainy rice
1 tablespoon Indian chutney

1 tablespoon minced candied orange peel
1 tablespoon grated coco-nut roasted
1 dessertspoon curry powder
2 oz. butter
1 oz. flour

1 quart water

Prepare and slice, or cut into cubes, the vegetables and apple, and fry them in the butter. Add the curry powder and the flour, and stir over the fire for a few minutes. Add the water (or vegetable stock), and bring slowly to the boil. Now add the remaining ingredients, except the rice, and let the soup simmer gently for an hour and a half. Ten minutes before serving add the cooked rice.

Sopa Español

2 onions, chopped fine
1 clove garlic, minced
½ lb. tomatoes, sliced
1 green pepper, diced
3 potatoes, diced
½ cup soaked green peas or Spanish peas

2 carrots, cut in strips
¼ cup pure olive-oil
1 tablespoon chopped black olives
1 oz. butter
Salt
Cayenne

Pour the oil into a large fireproof casserole, and when hot add the vegetables, and let cook gently until they begin to colour. Add one quart of water, the peas, and olives, and let simmer slowly for one hour.

Add fresh butter and seasoning, and serve.

The soup should be thick and rich, but may be diluted to taste.

Potage Bonne Femme

2 leeks	2½ oz. butter
4 small potatoes	Yolk of 1 egg
3 onions	1 gill milk
Heart of a small cabbage	1 teaspoon Marmite
1 cos lettuce	Salt
Pepper	

Cut the leeks lengthwise, and then into inch lengths. Slice the onions, and slowly stew both these in two ounces of the butter, without letting them brown. Add a quart of water, and the lettuce and cabbage, finely shredded, and the potatoes, thinly sliced, cover the saucepan, and let simmer gently for three-quarters of an hour.

Beat up the yolk with the milk, and pour the soup over, stirring gently. Add Marmite and seasoning.

Serve with zweiback.

Italian Rice Soup

2 onions	Milk
1 clove garlic	Grated Parmesan
½ lb. rice	Nutmeg
3 oz. butter	Pepper
Salt	

Chop the onions very fine, mince the garlic, and fry them together in the butter until slightly coloured. Add the dry rice, and cook for two or three minutes longer before adding one quart of water. Let cook gently, stirring to avoid burning, until the water is absorbed and the rice tender. Add rich boiling milk to the rice according to the thickness required. Season to taste, and serve with grated Parmesan.

Summer Soup

2 pints young peas	4 oz. mushrooms
4 young cucumbers	1 oz. butter
4 cos lettuces	1 teaspoon Marmite
3 young carrots	1 quart creamy milk
5 spring onions	Salt
1 sprig each of mint and parsley	Pepper

4

Slice or shred the vegetables and stew them with the peas and herbs in their own juice until tender. Add the milk, and simmer gently for ten minutes; then add Marmite and seasoning, and stir in the butter just before serving.

Onion Cream Soup

1½ lb. onions, Spanish and cooking mixed	6 peppercorns
	½ pint white breadcrumbs
2 oz. butter	1 gill cream
Salt	

Peel the onions, slice them thinly, and fry very gently in the butter without browning. When tender, add sufficient water, the salt, and the peppercorns, and simmer for forty-five minutes. Rub the onions through a sieve, and return the purée to the pan. Bring the cream to the boil, and pour it over the breadcrumbs. Add this to the soup, and serve as hot as possible.

Celery Cream Soup

2 heads celery	1 quart milk
½ onion	2 yolks of eggs
2 oz. butter	Salt
1 oz. flour	Pepper

Clean, trim, and cut the celery into small pieces. Slice the onion, and stir both together in the melted butter over a slow fire for three or four minutes. Add the flour, and stir for another minute or two. Moisten with the milk, and let simmer slowly until the vegetables are tender. Rub through a fine sieve, and return to the saucepan. Add the well-beaten yolks and seasoning, and heat without boiling. Serve.

Cream of Barley

2 oz. pearl barley	¼ teaspoon Marmite
1 pint milk	Salt
1 quart vegetable stock	Pepper
1 gill cream	Nutmeg
3 oz. butter	Pinch of brown sugar

Wash the barley, and bring it to the boil with the stock and seasoning, stirring occasionally. Add the milk, and let simmer gently for forty minutes.

Rub through a sieve, and return the barley to the saucepan. Bring to the boil again, add the Marmite, the cream (previously heated), sugar, and butter. Stir over a low fire until the butter melts, and serve.

Haricot Crème

½ lb. brown haricots	1 tablespoon seed tapioca
1 large Spanish onion	(powdered)
½ lb. cooking onions	Salt
3 oz. butter	Pepper
1 gill cream	Pinch of brown sugar

Soak the beans overnight. Slice and lightly fry the onions in the butter, and when coloured add the strained beans, and cook together for three minutes. Turn the whole into a stewpan with four pints of water, with the Marmite and sugar dissolved in it. Bring to the boil, and let simmer gently until the beans are quite tender. Put the whole through a fine sieve, and return the purée to the pan. Add the tapioca and cook for fifteen minutes before adding the cream.

Reheat and serve.

Potato Purée

½ lb. potatoes	1 pint milk
large Spanish onion	Yolks of 2 eggs
oz. butter	1 tablespoon tapioca
pint vegetable stock	Salt
	Pepper

Peel, slice, and cook the potatoes and onion in the butter without browning.

Add the stock (or water), bring to the boil, and let simmer until tender.

Rub the vegetables through a sieve, return to the

pan, add the milk, and boil. Now throw in the tapioca, and cook for eight or ten minutes. Add the yolks of eggs, reheat without boiling, and serve.

Cream of Spinach

½ pint cooked spinach	1 oz. flour
1 quart creamy milk	Salt
2 oz. butter	Pepper

Make a smooth white sauce of butter, flour, and milk.

Rub the spinach through a sieve, and add the purée to the sauce. Add seasoning, heat without boiling, and serve.

Haricot and Tomato Purée

1 lb. of tomatoes, or equivalent of tinned tomatoes	6 peppercorns
	2 teaspoons Demerara sugar
4 oz. white haricots	Tiny pinch of salt
1 shallot	Pepper
2 bouquets garnis	1 oz. butter

Soak the haricots overnight. Strain, and boil them until tender so that one quart of liquor remains. Add all the other ingredients, and let simmer gently until the whole will pass through a sieve easily. Return the purée to the saucepan, diluting with thin Marmite stock if too thick.

Heat thoroughly without boiling, and add the butter just before serving.

Cream of Cauliflower

1 large cauliflower	1½ pints milk
1 tablespoon butter	1 gill cream
1 pint stock	2 tablespoons fine ground rice
Salt and pepper to taste	

Soak the cauliflower in salted water for half an hour Cut into four sections, and boil until tender. Strain and reserve the water for stock. Rub the cauliflower through a sieve.

Slake the ground rice with a little cold milk, and bring it to the boil with the rest of the milk.

Add the cauliflower stock, the purée, and the seasoning, and bring all to the boil again. Let cook gently for five minutes, stirring.

Add the cream and the butter, reheat without boiling, and serve.

Cream of Artichoke

2 lb. Jerusalem artichokes	1 gill cream
1 head celery	1 oz. butter
2 onions	2 bay leaves
1 quart milk	3 peppercorns
	Seasoning

Peel the artichokes, and leave them to soak in water with a dash of lemon juice added.

Melt the butter in a saucepan, add half a cup of water, and put in the artichokes, onions, and celery stalks. Cover the pan, and leave the vegetables to steam very gently until tender.

Add the milk, and heat slowly without boiling. When hot, remove the onions and celery, rub the artichokes through a sieve, and return the purée to the saucepan. Add the seasoning, bay leaves, and peppercorns. Heat gently for half an hour more, without allowing to boil.

Remove the herbs, stir in the hot cream, and serve.

Green Pea Purée

2 pints shelled peas	1 oz. butter
The strung pods	½ gill cream
1 sliced onion	Yolk of 1 egg
2 sprigs mint	2 pints vegetable stock
1 bunch parsley	Salt and pepper to taste

Put the peas, pods, onion, and herbs in a stewpan with a quart of water. Boil until tender, and rub through a fine sieve. Return the purée to the pan, add the stock and butter, and cook gently for twenty

16

minutes. Remove the pan from the fire, and add the cream and yolk of egg.

Reheat without boiling, and serve.

Onion and Vermicelli

2 lb. onions
4 oz. butter
1 teaspoon brown sugar

3 oz. vermicelli
1 teaspoon Marmite
Salt
Pepper

Chop the onions small, and cook slowly in the butter to a pale golden colour. Turn them into a stewpan with two quarts of water, with the sugar added, and let cook gently until the onions are very tender. Strain off the broth, add the Marmite, seasoning, and cooked vermicelli.

Reheat, and serve with grated cheese.

Pot-au-Feu

1 lb. carrots
1 lb. small yellow swedes
3 leeks
1 onion stuck with cloves
1 parsnip
2 oz. soaked brown haricots
2 heads celery
2 oz. green peas

1 clove garlic
1 sweet apple
1 small cabbage
3 or 4 mushrooms
2 teaspoons Marmite
1 bouquet garni
6 peppercorns
Salt
Pepper

Put all the ingredients in a large stewpan with four or five quarts of water, and let simmer gently for four hours. Strain off the broth. Cut the vegetables into neat round pieces, and put in. Add little pieces of fresh butter, sprinkle with finely chopped parsley, and serve hot.

Tomato Soup (1)

1 lb. fresh tomatoes
1 small onion chopped fine
2 oz. butter
1 tablespoon flour
1 teaspoon brown sugar

½ gill cream
1 pint milk
1 pint boiling water
Salt
Pepper

Scald, peel, slice, and fry the tomatoes with the onion in the butter for five minutes. Add the water, and cook gently for thirty minutes. Strain, and rub through a sieve.

Make a smooth paste of the flour with a little of the cold milk. Add the rest of the milk to the soup, bring to the boil, and then add the paste. Cook for fifteen minutes.

Add the tomatoes, cream, and seasoning, reheat without boiling, and serve.

Tomato Soup (2)

1½ lb. ripe tomatoes	1 oz. butter
2 onions	1 tablespoon flour
1 leek	1 pint milk
1 carrot	Pepper
1 potato	Salt

Pinch of brown sugar

Scald, peel, and slice the tomatoes. Cut the vegetables small, and toss them lightly in the butter for two minutes.

Put the tomatoes and the fried vegetables in a stewpan with one quart of water, and let simmer gently for an hour and a half.

Rub through a sieve, and return to the pan. Add the flour, slaked with the milk, and cook gently for ten minutes without boiling.

Season, and serve.

Pine Kernel Soup

¼ lb. ground pine kernels	2 pints milk
¼ lb. chopped onions	¼ pint white haricot stock
2 oz. butter	3 tablespoons cream
2 tablespoons flour	Yolk of 1 egg

Seasoning.

Fry the onions and nuts in the butter until very lightly coloured. Add the flour, and stir for a minute or two. Then add the stock, and finally the milk. Bring to the boil, and let simmer gently for half an hour to thicken. Stir occasionally. Rub through a hair sieve, add the cream and well-beaten yolk of egg and seasoning.

Reheat without boiling, and serve.

Cream of Vegetable Marrow

3 lb. of fresh marrow
4 oz. butter
1 onion
1 quart milk

1 gill thick white sauce made with milk
1 teaspoon brown sugar
Seasoning to taste

Cut up, and stew the marrow and onion in half a pint of water, with the butter and sugar added.

When tender press through a sieve, return to the pan, and add the sauce and the milk.

Let boil gently for a few minutes, stirring to avoid burning.

Russian Bread Soup

4 crusts of wholemeal bread
5 oz. butter

1 lb. onions
Salt
Pepper

Butter the crusts, and bake them fairly dry in the oven as for zweiback.

Slice the onions, and fry them in four ounces of the butter. When slightly coloured add the bread broken into pieces. Cook until well browned, taking care to avoid burning. Add a quart of plain boiling water, allow to reboil, draw at once to one side, and let simmer gently for half an hour. Season to taste.

Consommé Julienne

2 carrots, cut in fine strips
½ lb. swede turnips, cut in fine strips
2 potatoes, cut in small balls with a vegetable scoop
1 leek cut in strips
¼ savoy cabbage, shredded
1 tablespoon cooked peas

1 onion, thinly sliced
1 small stick celery, in strips
1 teaspoon Marmite
2 tablespoons butter
Salt
Pepper
Pinch of sugar
2 quarts clear soup stock (see recipe)

Cut the vegetables into long thin strips, little balls, and shreds, and cook a little in the butter. Add the stock and seasonings, and simmer gently for about half an hour. Add the Marmite. Put in the peas five minutes before serving.

Crème Solferino

½ pint large split peas
2 leeks
2 onions
1 carrot
4 oz. yellow swede
1 oz. butter

½ head of celery (or 1 tea-spoon celery seed in a mus-lin bag)
1 gill cream (or rich milk)
Salt
Pepper

Pick and wash the peas, and put them in a stewpan with a quart of water. Bring slowly to the boil, and let simmer gently for two hours. Add the vegetables, cut or sliced, and let simmer for two more hours. Remove the scum, and strain the soup through a fine sieve.

Return the soup to the pan, add the butter and hot milk or whipped cream (if cream, it should be worked in gradually).

Season, reheat, and serve.

Lentil Cream Soup

Proceed as for Crème Solferino, using lentils in place of split peas.

Piquant Tomato Purée

1 tin tomatoes
½ stick celery
¼ small onion stuck with 2 cloves
1 bay leaf
2 chillies

4 peppercorns
2 tablespoons cooked peas
Yolks of 2 eggs
Salt
Cayenne
Pinch of sugar

1 pint clear vegetable stock

Put the tomatoes, celery, onion, and condiments in the stock, and let them cook gently for half an hour.

Put the liquid and the tomatoes through a sieve, return them to the pan, add the celery cut and shredded and the peas. Let simmer for five minutes.

Season, add the well-beaten yolks, and serve.

Chestnut Purée

1½ lb. chestnuts   1 gill cream
Milk   Ground mace
Cayenne

Slit and boil the chestnuts in plenty of water for ten minutes. Drain them, and remove the shells and skins. Stew them gently in water until tender, then mash and rub them through a fine sieve. Add hot milk until the desired thickness is obtained, season, and add the cream.

Reheat without boiling, and serve.

Fruit Consommé

1 quart clear soup stock (see   1 oz. sultanas
  recipe)   1 leek
¼ lb. large prunes   1 oz. butter
Almond balls (see recipe)

Soak the fruit in just sufficient water to cover. Cut the leek into julienne strips, and sauté them in the butter for about ten minutes. Add a little of the stock, and cook for a few minutes more before adding the rest. Put in the fruit and the almond balls, and simmer very gently for twenty minutes.

Serve the consommé with ground nuts.

Cream of Brazil Nut

¾ lb. ground Brazil nuts   1 oz. butter
3 mushrooms   1 oz. flour
2 onions   1 quart vegetable stock
1 gill cream

Chop the onions and the mushrooms fine, and fry them very slowly in the butter with the nuts added, colouring them no deeper than a pale yellow. Stir in the flour, and add by degrees the stock. Bring slowly to the boil, and simmer until the onions are tender. Pass the whole through a fine sieve, reheat, and add the cream just before serving.

Almond Cream Soup

3 oz. ground almonds	1 leek
1 oz. butter	1 pint vegetable stock
1 oz. flour	1 pint milk
1 onion	½ gill cream
Grate of nutmeg	

Chop the onion and leek very fine, and fry lightly in the butter without browning. Stir in the flour, cook for one minute, then add the almonds, stock, and milk by degrees. Bring to the boil, skim, then let simmer very slowly for forty minutes. Pass the soup through a sieve, reheat, and add the cream before serving.

Custard quenelles may be served with this soup.

Consommé Celestine

1 quart clear soup stock (see recipe)	2 eggs
2 oz. flour	1 teaspoon minced parsley
½ oz. grated cheese	1 teaspoon mixed herbs
2 tablespoons thick tomato purée	Salt
	Pepper
	1 oz. butter for frying

Make a batter of the ingredients (excepting stock). Let it rest for fifteen minutes, and fry as small pancakes. Cut these into the narrowest possible strips, place them in the tureen, and pour the hot stock over.

Serve with grated cheese.

Green Split Pea Soup

1 pint split green peas	1 sprig fresh mint (or 1 teaspoon dried mint)
1 small onion, chopped fine	
1 gill milk	Minced parsley to garnish
½ gill cream	Salt
	Pepper

Soak the peas overnight, drain, and sauté lightly in the butter with the chopped onion. Add one quart of boiling water, and let simmer gently for two hours. Pass through a sieve, water and all, return to the pan, add the milk, mint, and seasoning. Reheat and add the cream.

Before serving, sprinkle a little minced parsley over.

Bean and Vegetable Crème

½ lb. butter beans	1 gill milk
2 onions	¼ gill cream
2 mushrooms	½ teaspoon Marmite
1 small parsnip	Yolk of 1 egg
1 oz. butter	Salt
Pepper	

Soak the beans overnight in sufficient water to cover them. Wash them, add three pints of water, and set to boil gently for an hour and a half. After this time add the vegetables, previously cleaned and prepared, cut small, and fried pale brown in the butter. Continue to cook for one hour, after which strain and rub through a sieve.

Return the purée to the pan, add the milk with the egg yolk beaten up in it, and reheat very gently without allowing the soup to boil. Add seasoning and a little Marmite to taste, and finally the cream stirred in gradually.

The crème is then ready to serve.

Lentil and Parsnip Purée

½ lb. red lentils	1 oz. butter
1 onion	Yolk of 1 egg
1 parsnip	Pepper
1 tomato	Salt
1 gill milk	Nutmeg

Wash the lentils, and let them simmer gently for one hour in three pints of water. Meanwhile cut up and lightly fry the onion, parsnip, and tomato in the butter. When nicely coloured, moisten with a little of the lentil liquor, and turn into the pan with the lentils. Let boil gently for forty-five minutes. Rub through a sieve, and return to the pan. Add the milk with the egg yolk beaten up in it, reheat without boiling, and the purée is ready to serve.

Clear Vegetable Soup

1 small cabbage	1 parsnip
1 cauliflower	½ of a yellow swede
1 lb. onions (Spanish and cooking onions)	A few green stalks of celery
	2 dessertspoons tapioca
6 leeks	½ teaspoon Marmite
½ lb. carrots	Celery salt

Pepper

Clean, and cut the vegetables as fine as possible. Fry them until well coloured in one ounce of butter. Add five pints of water, bring slowly to the boil, and let simmer gently for four hours. Add the soaked tapioca, and continue to cook until the tapioca clears. Strain, add celery salt and pepper to taste, and a bare half-teaspoon of Marmite.

Garnish with custard or almond quenelles.

Butter Bean Consommé

½ lb. butter beans	2 oz. of yellow swede
1 lb. medium onions	2 or 3 green celery stalks
2 leeks	2 mushrooms
3 small carrots	1 bunch of parsley
6 brussels sprouts	1 oz. butter

Soak the beans overnight in sufficient hot water to cover. Add five pints of water, and let them boil gently for five or six hours.

Chop the vegetables, and fry them in a little butter, add the strained bean liquor, and let simmer for five hours. Strain through a scalded cloth. The soup is then ready to serve.

16

Lentil and Tomato (Clear)

1 lb. Egyptian lentils
½ lb. tomatoes or 1 small tin tomatoes
1 stick celery
4 cloves
1 bay leaf
6 peppercorns
1 tablespoon tapioca
Salt
Pepper

Wash the lentils until clean, and boil them with the sliced (or tinned) tomatoes, the celery, and spices in two quarts of water. When the lentils are tender (but not mushy), strain through scalded double muslin, taking care not to rub the lentils through. Let the soup settle, and pour off carefully, leaving the sediment (for use in gravies and sauces).

Put the soup in a stewpan with the tapioca, and boil gently until the latter is clear.

Split Pea and Tomato Purée

½ lb. yellow split peas
¾ lb. tomatoes
3 green celery stalks
2 onions
1 tablespoon flour
1 oz. butter
¼ teaspoon Marmite
1 gill milk
Celery salt and pepper to taste

Soak the peas overnight in a little more than enough water to cover them. Put them in a saucepan with a quart of water, and let boil gently for half an hour. Add the sliced vegetables, and cook until the peas are tender. Rub the whole through a sieve, and return to the pan.

Stir the flour in the melted butter for a minute or two, and then add to the purée.

Season, and add the milk, reheat without boiling, and serve.

Carrot and Rice Soup

2 lb. fine flavoured carrots
2 onions
1 leek (white part)
4 oz. boiled brown rice, grainy
Butter
2 quarts vegetable stock
1 gill milk
1 dessertspoon Demerara sugar
1 tablespoon cornflour
Salt
Pepper
Nutmeg

Wash and scrape the carrots, slice them, and put them with the sliced leek and the onions to stew gently in four ounces of butter. After three or four minutes add the stock and seasonings, and let the whole simmer until the carrots are tender.

Rub through a fine sieve, and return to the pan. Add the cornflour slaked in the milk. Stir, and let simmer for ten minutes, add the cooked rice, and cook five minutes more without boiling.

Spinach and Potato Soup

1 lb. potatoes	1 quart white stock (rice or
A handful of spinach	barley)
2 onions	1 gill milk
4 oz. butter	4 tablespoons cream
Yolks of 2 eggs	Seasoning

Peel and slice the potatoes and onions, and sauté them lightly in half the butter, without browning. Pour in the stock, and boil until the vegetables are tender. Rub through a sieve, and return to the saucepan. Shred the spinach, and cook until tender in the rest of the butter.

Heat the soup, stir in the milk, and add the yolks beaten with the cream. Stir until thickened, but the soup must not be allowed to boil.

Add the spinach and seasoning, and serve.

Carrot Crème Soup

1½ pints clear vegetable stock	Salt
Purée of 1 lb. cooked carrots	Pepper
1 tablespoon tapioca	Nutmeg
1 gill cream	Pinch of Demerara sugar

Crush the tapioca, and add to the boiling stock. Cook for ten minutes. Add next the carrot purée, and heat thoroughly.

Season, and stir in the cream, and the soup is ready to serve.

Dried Green Pea Soup

½ pint dried green peas
1 lettuce
2 handfuls of chopped spinach
½ onion, grated raw
2 sprigs mint, or 1 teaspoon
dried mint

1 bunch parsley
4 oz. butter
1 pint milk
½ gill cream
1 teaspoon Demerara sugar
Seasoning

Soak the peas overnight ; wash them and put to boil with the lettuce, onions, spinach, mint, parsley, sugar, and two ounces of butter. When tender, rub through a sieve, and return the purée to the pan.

Add the milk and seasoning, and reheat without boiling. Before serving add the cream, stirring it in by degrees.

White Soubise Soup

4 or 5 large onions
2 or 3 stalks of celery
1 pint cauliflower stock
1 pint milk
2 oz. butter

1 oz. flour
½ oz. cornflour
Salt
Pepper
Nutmeg

1 bay leaf

Chop the onions fine and toss them lightly in the melted butter over a low fire, so that they do not brown. Add the flour, and stir for another minute before adding the stock, gradually. Bring to the boil, and add the bay leaf and the finely chopped celery. Let simmer gently for one hour. Add seasoning.

Slake the cornflour with a little milk, add the rest of the milk, and pour into the soup. Cook for ten minutes more, stirring. Serve.

Children's Soup Lunch

1 onion
2 carrots
3 potatoes
1 bouquet garni
1 slice stale wholemeal bread,
diced

1 cup diced nutmeat
1 egg
1 oz. butter
1 dessertspoon Marmite
1 quart boiling water

Prepare and slice the vegetables, and brown them in the melted butter. Add boiling water and the herbs, and let simmer gently for forty-five minutes. Press through a sieve, return to the pan, and add the Marmite. Dust the diced bread and nutmeat with wholemeal flour, dip in beaten egg, and when well covered drop them into the soup.

Bring to the boil, and serve.

Fresh Fruit Soup

Mix equal quantities of strawberries, raspberries, and cherries (too small for dessert), stalked and stoned. Cook the fruit very slowly for half an hour in the required amount of water, with a pinch of Barbados sugar, nutmeg, and lemon flavouring added. Pass it all through a sieve, and reheat slightly.

Serve with stiffly whipped cream, and roasted hazel nuts, or chill and serve as fruit cup.

Cherry Soup

Cook fresh ripe cherries *very gently* in sufficient water with two or three cloves, a dash of cinnamon, and a grate of lemon rind. When tender, pulp through a sieve, return the purée to the pan, and cook slowly for ten minutes with a dessertspoon of brown sago.

Serve hot, in cups, or chilled as fruit cocktail with Welch's Grape Juice added.

Swedish Fruit Soup

¼ lb. prunes	1 tablespoon brown sago
¼ lb. dried apple rings	A stick of cinnamon
¼ lb. seedless raisins	1 teaspoon dark Barbados sugar

Wash and soak the prunes and the apple rings overnight in sufficient water to cover them. Add another quart of water, a small stick of cinnamon, and the brown sago. Let simmer very gently until tender. Remove the cinnamon, add sugar and almond balls before serving. Make the almond balls with one ounce of ground sweet almonds, a pinch of salt, sugar, and nutmeg, and sufficient egg to bind into a stiff paste. Roll into tiny balls, and drop them into hot butter for a minute. Drain, and put into the soup.

Purée of Leeks

1 dozen leeks	Milk
1 Spanish onion	Yolk of 1 egg
3 oz. butter	Seasoning
1 gill Béchamel sauce	Pinch of sugar
½ teaspoon Marmite	

Cut and shred the leeks, and stew them in the butter with the sliced onion until tender. Add the seasoning and a pinch of sugar, and the sauce, and cook for fifteen minutes.

Pass through a sieve, moistening at the same time with sufficient milk to give the desired consistency. Add the Marmite, and the egg yolk beaten in a little milk.

Reheat without boiling, and serve with grated cheese.

Cauliflower Purée

3 cauliflowers	½ gill cream
½ pint Béchamel sauce	Salt
½ pint barley or rice stock	Pepper
1 pint milk, scalded	Nutmeg
Yolk of 1 egg	Pinch of sugar

Break the cauliflowers into small pieces, put them into cold water, and bring them slowly to the boil. Drain, and make the sauce with the vegetable water, and put in the cauliflowers. Bring the sauce slowly to the boil, draw the pan to one side, and let simmer until the cauliflower is tender.

Rub the whole through a sieve, and moisten with

the stock at the same time. Add the scalded milk, and cook gently for a further ten minutes, stirring occasionally. Finally, add the yolk beaten with the cream, and reheat without boiling. Season to taste, and just before serving add a pat of fresh butter.

Barley Soup

2 oz. pearl barley	1 teaspoon wholemeal flour
2 onions	½ gill cream
2 carrots	1 pint milk
1 potato	1 yolk of egg
1 oz. butter	Seasoning

Soak the barley in lukewarm water for ten minutes. Prepare and slice the vegetables, and fry them lightly in the butter. Stir in the flour, and cook for a minute more. Gradually add a quart of water and the seasoning, stirring well. Bring to the boil, skim, and add the soaked barley, and let simmer gently for one hour.

Strain, and return the soup to a fresh saucepan ; add the yolk beaten up with the milk. Reheat, but do not boil the soup.

Add the cream, gradually stirring it in, just before serving.

Tomato and Potato Purée

1 lb. ripe tomatoes	1 small stick celery
1 large onion, chopped fine	3 oz. butter
¾ lb. potatoes	½ gill cream
1 carrot	Salt
Pepper	

Melt the butter in a stewpan, and gently stew the tomatoes and onion for fifteen minutes. Add three pints of water and the seasoning.

Prepare and cut the remaining vegetables small, and put them into the soup. Bring to the boil, and let simmer until pulpy. Pass through a sieve.

Reheat, season, and stir in the cream before serving. Serve with zweiback, or tiny wholemeal bread croûtons.

Cream of Oatmeal

4 oz. medium oatmeal	4 oz. yellow swede
1 carrot	2 oz. butter
1 onion	Milk as required
1 leek	½ gill cream

Cut up the vegetables, and sauté them lightly in the butter without browning them. Add one quart of water, and stir in the oatmeal with a wooden spoon. Mix well. Let simmer for two hours, stirring often, and diluting with hot water if too thick.

Press through a sieve, and return the purée to a clean pan. Add sufficient milk to bring the soup to the thickness of cream, and heat thoroughly. Just before serving add a delicate seasoning, and stir in the cream.

Serve with a crisp garnish.

Potage Parmentier

1½ lb. potatoes	½ pint milk
2 onions	¼ gill cream
2 leeks	1 oz. butter
3 peppercorns	Minced parsley
3 pints vegetable stock	Celery salt
	Paprika

Peel and slice the vegetables, and sauté them in the butter over a slow fire without browning. Add the stock and the peppercorns, and let simmer for an hour and a half.

Put the soup through a sieve, return to a clean pan, and add the milk and seasoning.

Reheat, and before serving stir in the cream.

Vermicelli Soup

1 quart vegetable stock	Yolk of one egg
2 leeks, white part	1 oz. butter
1 carrot	1 oz. vermicelli
1 bouquet garni	Pepper
½ teaspoon Marmite	Salt

Cut up the leeks and carrot, and fry them until about to colour in the butter. Turn the vegetables and the bouquet garni into the boiling stock, and let simmer for forty-five minutes.

Strain the liquid into a clean saucepan, bring to the boil, and throw in the vermicelli, broken small. Let simmer again until the vermicelli is tender. Beat up the yolk with a little of the soup, and add. Season to taste.

Add the Marmite, reheat gently, and serve.

White Crème Soup

2 potatoes	1 pint milk
2 onions	¼ gill cream
2 heads celery	1 pint rice stock
1 turnip	1 dessertspoon flour
1½ oz. butter	Seasoning

Cut up the vegetables, and sauté them lightly in the melted butter without browning them. Stir in the flour, and add by degrees the rice water. Bring to the boil, and let simmer gently for one hour, stirring occasionally.

Rub through a sieve, add the milk, and heat thoroughly without boiling. Season to taste, and just before serving stir in the cream.

Clear Green Lentil Soup

½ lb. green lentils	1 oz. butter
½ lb. onions	1 bouquet garni
1 oz. spinach leaves	3 dessertspoons crushed
1 small clove garlic	tapioca
4 or 5 nasturtium seeds	Salt
6 peppercorns	Pepper
Pinch of Cayenne.	

Chop and fry the onions in the butter until lightly browned. Add the lentils, spinach, herbs, and two quarts of water. Bring slowly to the boil, and let simmer gently for two hours.

17

Strain off the liquid, and allow to settle ; then pour off carefully, leaving the sediment (which may be used in other dishes). Add the tapioca to the liquor, and let boil gently until clear. Season to taste.

Garnish this soup with rich quenelles.

Dutch Onion Soup

1½ lb. onions	1½ pints water
3 oz. butter	4 peppercorns
2 yolks of eggs	½ teaspoon Marmite
2 tablespoons flour	Grated Dutch cheese
1 pint milk	Salt
	Pepper

Chop and sauté the onions lightly in two ounces of butter for four or five minutes. Rub through a sieve.

Melt the rest of the butter, stir in the flour, and add by degrees the milk, previously scalded, the peppercorns, and seasoning. Cook this sauce for five minutes, stirring constantly. Then pour it into the onion soup, and let the whole simmer for fifteen minutes, stirring frequently. Add the Marmite. Beat the yolks of the eggs, and stir in (off the fire).

Reheat cautiously, and serve with a sprinkling of grated cheese.

Scotch Broth

2 oz. pearl barley	6 oz. nutmeat in half-inch
2 large onions	dice
2 oz. yellow swede in small	2 oz. butter
dice	1 bouquet garni
2 carrots	2 teaspoons Marmite
3 leeks	Celery salt
	Pepper

Toss the barley in a little melted butter for three or four minutes, and throw it into two quarts of boiling water. Let cook slowly.

Cut the carrots into small sticks. Slice the onions and the leeks. Fry the vegetables in the rest of the butter until slightly coloured, add them to the broth, and let simmer gently for two hours. Add seasoning to taste, and the Marmite.

Just before serving add the nutmeat, previously tossed in a little butter.

Stock for Clear Soup

1 lb. butter beans	1 teaspoon celery seed
1 head celery	1 teaspoon mixed dried herbs
½ lb. onions	1 bay leaf
2 leeks	4 peppercorns
½ lb. carrots	3 oz. butter
½ yellow swede	Salt
1 bunch parsley	Pepper

Soak the beans overnight in sufficient water to cover them.

Slice and cut up the vegetables and fry them in the butter. Turn them into a stewpan with the beans, and the herbs tied up in muslin, and five pints of water. Bring slowly to the boil, and let simmer for three hours.

Strain through a fine sieve, season, and use as required.

Vegetable Stock

1 carrot, 3 oz.	1 potato, 3 oz.
1 leek	1 tablespoon barley

Slice the vegetables, add a quart of water, bring to the boil, and let simmer gently for one hour.

Strain, and use as directed.

Barley Stock

3 oz. barley	1 grated onion
	3 pints water

Bring slowly to the boil, skim, and let simmer gently for one hour.

Strain, and use as directed.

Use rice or macaroni water for the same purpose.

To clarify Clear Soups

When clear soups are required, translucent and sparkling, add to each quart of cooled soup the white of an egg, slightly beaten with the crushed shell. Bring the soup slowly to the boil, stirring the while. Now let the soup continue to boil for five minutes, but do not stir during this period. Add four tablespoons of cold water (as for settling coffee grounds), and let stand for a few minutes to settle.

Strain the soup through double muslin, and serve.

SAUCES

ACCORDING to the French, from whom all culinary blessings flow, the cooking and roasting of things is difficult but not impossible, and in the opinion of the much-quoted Brillat-Savarin, " it needs genius to make a sauce."

It is as well to know, however, that the chief French sauce is Spanish : Sauce Espagnole. The secret of Spanish sauce is the browning of the flour, the careful roasting of which in the making of the roux develops the rich colour and characteristic smoked flavour. Once this is grasped, the inventive cook will find no difficulty in preparing the whole range of brown sauces, savoury, piquant, or bland. Of these, as the French say, Sauce Espagnole is the " parent."

Opposite Sauce Espagnole is the foundation white sauce—Béchamel—for which the flour is not browned, but blended with the butter and carefully cooked to a velvety smoothness before the milk or liquid is added. The addition of egg yolks and cream to this basic white sauce gives Sauce Allemande. Mushroom or haricot liquor added to white sauce enriched with a little cream gives Sauce Velouté. In the same way any special addition will yield a correspondingly typical sauce.

The alternative methods of sauce making may be tabulated as :

(1) Melt the butter in a saucepan, stir in the dry flour, and cook until frothy, stirring meanwhile. Gradually add the liquid, hot or cold, still stirring, and cook until thick and smooth.

(2) Rub the butter and flour together and stir into

261

the warm liquid in a double cooker, and continue to cook and stir until thick and smooth.

For *thin* white sauce use one tablespoon of fat and one tablespoon of flour to half a pint of liquid.

For *thick* sauce use two to four tablespoons of fat, and three to four tablespoons of flour to half a pint of liquid. This forms a useful basis for soufflés and croquettes.

For *medium* sauce use two tablespoons of flour and two tablespoons of fat to half a pint of liquid.

For an improvised Sauce Hollandaise add the beaten yolks of two eggs to half a pint of white sauce and cook in a double boiler, as for custard. Flavour with a tablespoon of lemon juice and a trace of nutmeg.

Sauce Béchamel

2 oz. butter	1 carrot
1½ oz. flour	6 peppercorns
1 pint scalded milk	1 blade mace
¼ pint mushroom liquor	1 bay leaf
1 onion	Sprig of parsley
	Salt

Grate the carrot and the onion raw, and put them to boil with the milk and stock, adding the herbs. Melt the butter in another pan, and stir in the flour, cooking lightly for one minute over a very low fire. Remove the mace and bay leaf, and add the milk to the butter and flour, stirring to blend smoothly. Bring to the boil, and let simmer for twenty minutes. Remove the parsley, and pass the sauce through a sieve. Season, and use as directed.

Sauce Espagnole

2 oz. flour	1 large tomato
2 oz. butter	3 mushrooms
1½ pints haricot stock (or vegetable stock)	2 bouquets garnis
	6 peppercorns
1 onion	1 teaspoon Demerara sugar
1 shallot	Pepper
	Salt

Put the vegetables, cut small, with the herbs in a
ewpan containing the melted butter, and cook until
icely browned (avoid scorching). Stir in the flour
nd cook gently for a further three minutes. Add the
:ock gradually. Bring slowly to the boil, and let
immer for at least thirty minutes. Strain through a
air sieve,and the sauce is ready.

A little sherry may be added during cooking.

Sauce Velouté

To three-quarters of a pint of Béchamel sauce add,
just before serving, quarter gill of cream, stirring it
well in, and a trace of nutmeg.

Sauce Allemande

Use three-quarters of a pint of Béchamel sauce as a
basis. Beat up the yolks of two eggs with two tablespoons of cream, add to the sauce, and stir over a low
fire until the yolks begin to set. Do not let the sauce
boil.

Add lemon juice to taste, and a pinch of nutmeg
before serving.

Sauce Maintenon

½ pint Béchamel sauce	Yolks of 2 small eggs
½ oz. butter	1 small onion
½ oz. grated Parmesan	Salt
Pinch of Cayenne	

Chop the onion, and fry in the butter without browning. Add the Béchamel, and let boil for twenty
minutes, stirring constantly. Strain into a clean
saucepan, add the well-beaten yolks (off the fire), cook
over a low fire, and stir until it thickens. Do not let
the sauce boil. Then stir in the cheese, season, and
serve.

Melted Butter Sauce
(Sauce Anglaise)

1 oz. butter	¾ oz. flour
	½ pint cold water

Melt the butter in a scrupulously clean pan, sift in the flour, and stir over a low fire until the flour is absorbed and a smooth paste results. Add gradually the cold water, stirring it in steadily. Pass through a fine strainer if necessary. Just before serving, half an ounce of fresh butter and a squeeze of lemon juice may be added. Season to taste.

Boiling milk may be used instead of water.

Note.—If the sauce lumps while the water is being added, beat smooth with a wooden spoon until the sauce boils. Let it boil for twelve or fifteen minutes to ensure the perfect cooking of the flour, stirring occasionally.

Sauce Piquant

¾ pint Sauce Espagnole	1 teaspoon chopped nasturtium seeds
1 dessertspoon chopped gherkins	2 shallots
1 dessertspoon chopped capers	1 tablespoon butter
	3 tablespoons vinegar

Put the capers, gherkins, and nasturtium seeds with the vinegar, and simmer gently until the vinegar is reduced by half.

Chop the shallots fine, and brown them in the butter. Add the capers, gherkins, etc., to the sauce, and add the shallots. Heat thoroughly before serving.

Brown Flour Sauce

1 oz. wholemeal flour	1 carrot
1½ oz. butter	1 green stalk of celery or celery salt
1 bouquet garni	
1 onion	Seasoning
	Four-fifths of a pint of water

31

Melt the butter in a saucepan, and brown the thinly sliced vegetables in it. Stir in the flour, and cook over a low fire until lightly coloured (avoid scorching). Add the water gradually, stirring well. Add herbs, bring slowly to the boil, and let simmer for rather more than one hour.

Strain, reheat, add seasoning, and use as required.

Wholemeal Cheese Sauce

1 oz. grated Parmesan	1 saltspoon made mustard
1 oz. grated Cheddar	½ pint milk
2 tablespoons wholemeal flour	2 tablespoons cream
1 oz. butter	Seasoning

Melt the butter, stir in the wholemeal flour, and cook lightly for one or two minutes. Add the milk, stirring well, and the seasonings. Bring slowly to the boil, and let simmer gently for fifteen minutes. Dilute if too thick with a little hot milk.

Stir in the cheese, and add the cream before serving.

Sauce Hollandaise

4 yolks of eggs	Juice of ½ a lemon
2 oz. butter	A trace of nutmeg
Pepper and salt to taste	

Melt a little of the butter in a small saucepan, add the seasoning, and the egg yolks, and place it in another pan of hot water over a low fire. Stir well with an egg whisk, and add the butter a small piece at a time, working each addition in thoroughly. Stir over a low fire long enough for the yolks to thicken, taking great care to keep the sauce below boiling point.

Strain the sauce, and add the lemon juice previously strained.

Sauce Italienne

½ pint Sauce Espagnole	Mushroom trimmings
1 medium onion	1 oz. butter
½ gill vegetable stock	1 small glass white wine
2 shallots	Seasoning
1 clove garlic	Pinch of Cayenne

Peel and finely chop the onion, shallots, mushrooms, and garlic. Sauté them in the melted butter for two or three minutes without colouring. Add the wine and the stock, and let simmer until reduced by a fourth. Stir in the sauce, and simmer for ten minutes.

Strain, season, and serve.

Tomato Sauce

¾ lb. tomatoes	1 clove garlic
1 small onion finely chopped	1 teaspoon Demerara sugar
½ oz. butter	Salt
1 bay leaf	Pepper

Sauté the onions in the butter, add the cut tomatoes and other ingredients, and let simmer gently for twenty minutes. Pass the sauce through a sieve, return to the pan, and let simmer until reduced to the desired consistency.

Egg Sauce

A hard-boiled egg, cut into small dice, mixed with half a pint of Béchamel sauce.

Sauce Suprême

½ pint butter bean stock	1½ oz. butter
½ gill cream	1 tablespoon flour
3 peppercorns	1 bouquet garni
2 small mushrooms	Salt

Melt half the butter, stir in the flour, add the stock, and bring to the boil. Add the mushrooms, herbs, peppercorns, and salt. Let simmer gently for half an hour.

Strain the sauce into another saucepan, add the cream, stirring over the fire, but not boiling.

Add the rest of the butter, off the fire, very little at a time, and allowing each addition to melt and be incorporated.

Sauce Maître d'Hôtel

Gradually beat two or three ounces of butter into
.alf a pint of Béchamel sauce, previously allowed to
immer with a little water until reduced in quantity.
Jow rub the sauce through a fine strainer or sieve, add
. teaspoon of minced parsley and two tablespoons of
emon juice.

Sauce Mornay

· pint Béchamel sauce	1 oz. butter
gill vegetable stock	½ gill cream
: oz. grated dry cheese	Salt
Pepper	

Heat the sauce and the stock, and let simmer until
·educed by one-quarter. Stir in the cream, and
gradually add the cheese, stirring it carefully into the
sauce. Add the seasoning, and remove the pan from
:he fire. Now add the butter, a little piece at a time,
seeing that each piece melts and is blended before
adding the next. Serve.

Browned Onion Sauce

Chop two onions finely, and brown them in an ounce
of butter. Add half a pint of water and seasoning, and
simmer slowly for fifteen minutes.

Rub through a sieve, reheat, and serve.

Black Butter Sauce

1 teaspoon finely minced parsley	2 oz. butter
	½ teaspoon vinegar

Fry the butter until nut brown, add the vinegar and
parsley, and pour directly over the dish with which it
is to be served—hard-boiled eggs, haricots, or potatoes.

Parsley Sauce

To half a pint of Béchamel sauce or melted butter
sauce add 1 dessertspoon of finely minced parsley and
a few drops of lemon juice.

Sauce Soubise

1¼ lb. onions   ½ gill creamy milk
1 cup Béchamel sauce   Seasoning

Cut the onions in half and boil them in the milk. When tender, drain free of milk, sieve them, and add to the Béchamel. Reheat, stir in the cream and seasoning, and serve.

Sauce Poulette

Make half a pint of white sauce with liquor in which mushrooms have been cooked.

Garnish with chopped mushrooms, previously sautéd in butter.

Caper Sauce

Mix a tablespoon of capers and half a tablespoon of vinegar with half a pint of melted butter sauce.

Note.—Make brown caper sauce with a brown sauce, chopped capers, and a seasoning of black pepper. Pickled or fresh nasturtium seeds in place of capers yield an agreeable result.

Sauce Robert

½ pint brown sauce   1 gill strained tomato pulp
1 onion   3 tablespoons sherry
1 oz. butter   1 saltspoon dry mustard
                              Salt

Chop the onion fine, and fry slightly in the butter. When coloured, stir in the dry mustard and the sherry. Heat thoroughly, and add the tomato pulp and the brown sauce. Let simmer for ten minutes, and the sauce is ready to serve.

Cream Sauce

Let half a pint of white sauce cook a little longer than usual. When reduced in quantity, add, just before serving, four tablespoons of fresh cream.

Do not boil the sauce after this addition.

Sauce Bearnaise

3 oz. butter	2 tablespoons onion juice
4 yolks of eggs	2 tablespoons tarragon vinegar
½ teaspoon chopped parsley	3 crushed peppercorns
½ teaspoon chopped tarragon	Salt
Pepper	

Cream the butter with a fork until quite soft. Put the egg yolks and seasonings into the upper pan of a double boiler, and beat them light with an egg-beater. Add the butter in three or four portions, beating each one in carefully before adding more. When perfectly smooth, add the onion juice and the vinegar, beating these well in. Now place the pan over boiling water, and cook for three minutes, stirring constantly.

Take the pan from the fire, add the herbs, and serve immediately.

Apple and Onion Sauce

1 large Spanish onion	1 tablespoon tarragon vinegar
1 large Bramley or similar apple	1 clove
	1 peppercorn
3 tablespoons butter	A little wholemeal flour
Seasoning	

Chop the onion fine, and sauté lightly in the butter. When half done, add the apple, washed and thinly sliced, without peeling or coring. Cook for two minutes, and stir in sufficient flour to make a thick paste. Cook until brown, stirring well, and dilute with water to a thin sauce. Add the vinegar and seasoning, and boil for five minutes.

Rub through a sieve, reheat, and serve.

Currant Jelly Sauce

3 oz. currant jelly	1 bay leaf
½ oz. butter	2 tablespoons lemon juice
1 tablespoon flour	3 gills vegetable stock
1 small onion	1 saltspoon celery salt

Lightly colour the chopped onion in the butter, stir in the flour, add the bay leaf and celery salt, and cook until browned. Add the stock and lemon juice, and let simmer for half an hour. Strain, add the jelly, and stir over a low fire until blended.

Curry Sauce

3 tablespoons butter	¾ pint vegetable stock
1 tablespoon flour	1 tomato
2 tablespoons finely chopped onion	1 teaspoon chopped parsley
	Salt
1 teaspoon curry powder	Pepper

Sauté the onion in the hot butter until nicely browned. Stir in the flour and the curry powder, and gradually add the stock, then the diced tomato and the parsley.

Bring to the boil, add the seasoning, and let cook gently for twenty minutes, stirring frequently. Strain, and serve hot or cold with vegetables, eggs, etc.

Apple Chantilly

½ cup mayonnaise	1 tablespoon grated horse-radish
½ cup stewed apple	
2 tablespoons cream	1 dessertspoon grated raw beetroot

Add the horse-radish and beetroot to the mayonnaise, stir in the apple sauce, mix well, and add, lastly, the cream.

Chill, and serve.

Italian Tomato Sauce

1 sliced carrot	2 tablespoons butter
1 sliced onion	2 tablespoons flour
1 finely chopped shallot	½ cup vegetable stock
1 bouquet garni	1 cup thick tomato purée
1 clove garlic, minced fine	Salt
2 cloves	Pepper
Trace of nutmeg	

Put the vegetables, herbs, and butter in a saucepan, and simmer for fifteen minutes.   Stir the flour into the tomato purée, add the stock, and stir again before pouring into the saucepan containing the vegetables.

Let simmer gently for one hour, strain, season, and use as required.

www.ingramcontent.com/pod-product-compliance
Ingram Content Group UK Ltd.
Pitfield, Milton Keynes, MK11 3LW, UK
UKHW040821230925
8033UKWH00021B/93

9 781447 408130